flipped eye publishing

The Wolf Who Cried Boy

simple words, rendered sublime

lol, for y... ...rative,
you p... ...l justice,
and f... ...n and
bec... ...ng,
Thankyou.

You've been such an amazing
support + friend to me this
year.
I saw this poet
+ thought
yev'd
appreciate
him!

All my love,
Hannah x

CW00553066

The Wolf Who Cried Boy
flipped eye publishing
www.flippedeye.net

First Edition
Copyright © Ainsley Burrows, 2008
Cover Image © Marbre Stahly, 2007
Cover Design © flipped eye publishing, 2008

ISBN-10: 1-905233-06-X
ISBN-13: 978-1-905233-06-9

British Library Cataloguing in Publication Data
A catalogue record for this book is available from the British Library

Editorial work for this book was supported by the Arts Council of England

Printed and Bound in the United Kingdom

Supported by
The National Lottery®
through Arts Council England

The Wolf Who Cried Boy

Ainsley Burrows
2008

to all the people who die or suffer when political men mislead

The Wolf Who Cried Boy

Contents

Dispatches

The Negro Unplugged

I am the negro unplugged;
I am Toby and Tiger Woods
crucified to the speed of light.
My telepathy is on the floor
of a methadone clinic
injecting the ace of spades spaded.

I am the knife in Caesar's back,
the bullet through Kennedy's face;
I am Jheri Curl juice
and hog-maws;
Sambo with his eardrums stolen;
fried chicken
dressed in nightmares and flames.
I am the never-not–never,
the always-not, not
I-be-who–I-say-I-is
because I am
a Slave ship in the middle
of the Sistine Chapel. I am Stepin Fetchit
wearing blue prints of the constitution
dying a death so beautiful.

I suffer with my eyes
closed, in blindfolds, gold
fronts fronting because I have
to survive this constant Christing.

Massacred martyr us be;
hence the thus, therefore, I am
Toussaint L'Overture

fractured,
hammered to the sky, French
doors and all,
1804 and all;
I am Harriet, Condoleeza
rice field, cane field, corn
row, Afro. I am the perm
the Conk, the weave
and the pressing iron –
irreligious and sacred, like
Garvey's bones on display
at the Louvre; I am Jimi Hendrix
guitar plugged into the ocean floor,
galactic high hat,

snare
kick drum,
kick drum,
snare

spirit gentrified to Picasso;
I am a double-headed cubist in the belly
of ten shredded tomorrows; I am
tomorrow yesterday,
a burning church inside
the whites only water fountain,
a metal dream, a song so
bitter,
we split the atom,
the black
Baghdad,
the Moorish now
Beirut on

a cotton gin
facing his inquisitors.

I am face paint and tribal scars,
crack pipe and tribal scars, track
marks and tribal scars, Harvard
and tribal scars; I am Dubois
old, wrinkled, wearing the Black Star
Liner around his neck
to Lincoln's assassination;
I am Malcolm at a Starbucks
in Harlem, the espresso machine
making love to my bullet wounds;
I am a blind musician
with no song to sing; I am
the black resistance, dreaming
of white girls with flowing hair –
like Rapunzel and Snow
White and Sleeping Beauty.
(Michael, wake up: the American
mind game has rearranged your face.)
I am a bottle of bleaching cream
poured into the palms of Jack
Johnson; I am genocide
in every Lyric that Big wrote:
I've been in this game for years
it made me an animal.
There is rules to this shit
I wrote me a manual;
I am the Rolling Stones
The Beatles, Bob Dylan
and Elvis Presley all in black
face; I am the Black psyche,

one eyed mouth of blood
whispering womb juice
into the fabric of Old Glory;
I am a black boy on a street corner
in Brooklyn, freestyling his way
back to God.

Black Boy

He's a street corner, a stoop
a blindfolded blunt, a nuclear
bomb in the middle of Brooklyn,
a thunderclap in the womb of death.
A black boy, a tranquilized metaphor,
the twice ghettoed, shackled
to the midnight in his hands,

shooting hoops, shooting off
at the mouth, middle Passage
in his cornrows, maps back
to the interior, back to Shango
back to the spirits.
Multidimensional black boy:
cotton seeds, tobacco sheds,
apartheid, Jim Crow, church
boy, field hands, crossover
like time travel in slave ship
Tenements. He's a fifth of vodka,
the black requiem, lost in fragments
of its own genius. He is government
cheese and divinity, food-stamps
and infinity; immune to the cyanide
in the quarter water.

The heat translates this dark boy
into a small song, into a canvas
of spilled insanity, into the chaos
trapped in a star's heartbeat.
This conjured oblivion,
this resistance of the dark

boy with his scrawny arms –
the sagging pants, scarlet
eyes squeezed tight
by cannabis;
seeds of confusion,
the perfume of wasted years
in his collar bone.

He's addicted
to street corners and malt liquor,
addicted to the taste
of his forefathers sweat in the tobacco
leaves; all that Hennessy, dreaming
beneath his tongue, next to the razor,
next to the history of ancestors
planted below Wall Street
the memories of a father
he's never seen, and he wants
to go places
so he's writing his name
on everything
that moves. Penned his greatest verse
on the window of a train, watched it
slide off into the killing twilight:
dear world,
what have I done
for you to hate me so?

He's a black buffalo, walking
backwards through the wheat.
Survivor of a million
noosed philosophies, Africa choked
from his acoustics, a dying world

on his face – poplar splints
from sea to shining blindness.
He was born invisible
with a tornado smile.
And Shango can't save him
from these men
who pray to the turbine
and the jet engine,
to their cell phones
and their murdered minks,
to their satellites
and their news briefs,
but he doesn't care.

He's a street corner, a stoop,
a blindfolded blunt,
a nuclear bomb
in the middle of Brooklyn,
a thunderclap in the womb of death.
A black boy,
a tranquilized metaphor,
the twice ghettoed
shackled to the midnight
in his hands.

Magnus

Black Magnus
The drum omega
blue-black mutation
of a transfigured Christ
Etched messiah of
the darker dark
cosmic graffitist
You wear your genocide well
ye sellers of frankincense and satellites
of walking scars
and nuclear comas
the fast food of history
racing through your square hearts
Concoctors of visibility
Malt liquor slingers
of the concrete noose
Dream stealers chained
to a visionless arithmetic
ain't no future in dead flags
or un-reincarnated suns

Magnus
hollowed through and through
with folded wombs to ponder
asses to classify
thighs to congratulate
and smack
you ventriloquist
of America's greatest fears
prophet you could have
be you is

a rebellion waiting
in the lock-jawed biting
of a wired mouth
speak Magnus speak
tilt your flask
or fall upon your sword
double crossed by
thirteen stripes of amnesia
Magnus
your silence is uncanny
Speak Magnus
dream and see
flail and flash scream and conjure
Magnus,
let the stars hear you dreaming
pour out your arms
and re-dream the world
retrieve the nightmares
of bullets whistling our children's names
dream these coffins back to trees
what if, Magnus,
what if you were our last hopes
you, didact of our prayers?
our stone pilled messiah
three thousand years removed
Magnus, your ancestors dreamt you flying

Torres

Have you seen the President's daughters
with their newly renovated faces
sipping Hollywood from the beautiful
womb of commerce? Is their corporate god
guiding your gun tonight, the desert
paralyzed by your silence,
Banquo's blood,
ignited boy,
Stained glass; afraid?

Torres you are a suit's fool,
a gospelled whorehouse,
a boulevard of songs excavated
from the howling flesh of a bluesman
believer. Didn't you hear the nuanced
catastrophe in the president's speech?
See the silos of warships
piled into his eyes? Speech that
orphaned your mother, left her
snapshots of the Viet Cong wearing
your father's smile: him drugged mechanical;
you infected by the rabies of oil
men, beckoned by the blinding franchise
of adolescence. Torres, nineteen,
have you ever seen an oil well? Where
is your heart? Is it somewhere
in the Jim crowed South Bronx?
In Ponce? In Viequez? In Washington
wandering the halls of iron and ice?

Torres, did the Iraqi women clutch
their purses, the way they clutch their children;
like errors on the landscape? How many
Iraqi babies does it take to fill your gas
tank? Torres, when the bullets kiss you
open, will you think about your mother;
the smell of fresh roses napalmed
into your carcass; your legs torn off
under a street sign you will never understand?

Torres, do you dream
in landmines, do you get flashes
of you turned inside out, your organs
hanging dark and heavy, covered
in CNN stock quotes and Islam,
the magnolia scented palms
of Texas down the barrel of your soul,
Nixon Vietnamed into your breast
Bone – dog tag musical Saigon
of sand, the helicopters like
background singers, violins weeping
tender? Now weep, Torres, weep
for all the ghosts of history,
for every nineteen year old
boy with a gun, from here to Macchu
Picchu, for every silent poet,
for the makers of uniforms.
Weep for every broken American
glued to the blue light;
weep for yourself, Torres,
because this poem is not for you;
this poem is for your mother.

Sheeple

Sound bite children, brainwashed
the sun. The next holocaust
is in the screensaver: microchip
the cross thread of history, a Wolfowitzian
future grown from Anthrax and five
Planes – Machiavellian Charlemagne.
The towers must go!

Forty thieves with Texan blood murmurs.
Star spangled freeze tag, toe tag, body
bag brilliance, blood baths and nuclear
shivers. And Jesus was there
moon-walking on water
911 tied to a tapped phone; was the president listening?
White horse on the white house lawn,
Prozac Jerusalem, road map to death
trap, Plutonium cloud on a knit shirt…
It's a corporate conspiracy, It's a corporate
cover up: they're shredding soldiers
again, fighting over land when they can't live
forever. There is a Nazi camp in Dick
Cheney's pace-maker: silent, secret, American
Gestapo dressed in Soviet news reels,
the Bay of Pigs and JFK
was Julius Caesar, so lift the evidence
from Jackie-O's hair-do and teach the babies
how to run, teach them to how to salute
at funerals. Because Jimi Hendrix is in the Congo
transporting drums back to Brooklyn.

The truth will give you an anaphylactic

shock Psychics and magnetic fields under
the Pentagon; 6000 years of secret handshakes
hidden in the shape of a building.
And Lady Liberty is riding a red camel
across a sky dyed coincidental: blood
hounds and war planes in the fine
print, and the west is playing Tantric
Russian roulette with Persia Minor, trying to get
their hands on Nebuchadnezzar's tomb,
on the blue prints to a star gate, wrestling
space probes out of a Muslim child's dream.

Pregnant princesses, car crashes
through French tunnels, Paparazzi
Assassins dipped in queens milk;
the twentieth century was a metaphor
drowning in the collapse of dream
collapsed in the suicide of memory.

Pretend

Let's pretend we didn't leave
codes in rivers, in collard greens
gumbo, grits; a parallel universe
hallucination of Garvey, wrapped
in barbed wire, whispering remedies
in the Harlem of our blood and sweat
curdled on leg irons throat shackles...

Bleed me a history book
of granulated sugar and cotton
gins, of smoke huts and crushed
spines, of African souls on European
pallets. MIT and Harvard can explain
nuclear fission, but they can't explain
the Harlem shake. Atlantic fever,

Goree Island gone mad; broke his neck
twelve times in twelve different places.
He's a zodiac sign on Ritalin,
a galaxy with a speech impediment
hand cuffed to a night-stick.
And most of our magicians were
murdered during the middle passage

because most of our magicians took
their drums on board. A small caption
in an even smaller room: "for sale,
two negroes and a drum." A drum
that bends space, reorganizes reality;
watch time mutate, rock and roll:
slave ships, funky dungeons, beat box

break
beat
back
beat
broken

backs sweating out tobacco stains,
scatting until our cells divided
blue. Let's swing –
swing until our mothers remember
swing until our children remember
that, "hip hop" was invented
by white men in slave quarters;

remember the unreported rapes,
the unreported uprisings, remember that
there are star systems in our spirit
that it is possible to dream even
when you are dead,
there are remnants of futures
in the conscience of your blood

tapping vision into wood. We suffered
in silence; guitars on fire, fists in the air
we howled and screamed until our gums bled
burning crosses and vacant lunch counters.
We'll return encrypted feedback
like a slave ship crashed into the Pentagon.
Disaster comes blind

like nineteen thousand light years
dressed in red, making promises to Wall Street:
you may find a stock quote

in a raindrop, helicopters in the flu
shot, war planes in a tear drop; pretend,
but just remember that we can't forget because
we are ninety percent liquid

and
ninety
nine
percent
space.

Presidents

Theroretical presidents, oil moguls
and military industrialists making calls
to the Black Sea. Cuban cigars.

Bloody Ben Franklin's throat
slit from ear to shining ear,
Confederate flags, abandoned skulls and bones.

Nazi Rumsfeld. Strauss in the popcorn,
Reagan playing his part again,
Star of David drawn on Arafat's back.

Cancer machined. Castro's fall. Russian
Coca Cola. Osama smuggling
America back into America

An opium of truth in the eye;
truth in the truth in his lies.
Snap shots from space. Swastika

dreams for the bible belt. Red states
shaped like Auschwitz,
like a nuclear god with a Tsunami prescription.

Three blind men shadowing,
boxing the head lines, head
lines, fist fighting theTV

John Walker trapped in Timothy's lunch
box. Seven starving children eating
land mines; a picture perfect future,

a future pictured perfect.
A presidential tear slides down
the President's face, turns

the presidential heart
into a presidential waste.
How beautiful!

Blind West

Look at the west
entangled in their formulaic
Kleptomania,
with their nuclear families
assembly line enlightenment
donating their children
to the chopping block
to the mechanical muscle of madness

Infectus americus,
frock of fascism,
fabricate a truth for us
pry it, flesh first,
from the incubus of our forgetfulness
lest we remember
that we too are human
that there is a two year old girl
in Fallujah – a corporation
has just purchased her ovaries

Wall street merchants
clutched in the nebris
of international pedophilia
an inevitable date rape
gone right.
Gentrified middle east
9th century kickbacks of
religious pornography.
A lab rat giving birth
to a nuclear bomb
bitter the blood of Byzantium

chemical news briefs
intoxicate us with trivia.
When a civilization dies
who does the autopsy?

Trivia;
we need it like a spoon of death
pump us full of the chaos
of the American goose step.
All hail the Nazi dollar.
The village idiot
and his entourage of kill-men
all church and god eyed
circus paint and method acting
precision killing and freedom pills
dress rehearsals and victory gin.
We need a tragedy
an assassin perched
someone not blinded
by the consumer friendly deaths
of young boys.
Spinsimple, we
ignore the flags
their mothers plant,
drape their coffins
in our socially engineered silence
because psychological suicide
has never been this easy.

Flags

I see a sea of fallen soldiers
Men too brave to cry
Men who shamelessly
Die for country
With their hands
Over their hearts
Reciting graves

I see them
Breathing the lonely stars
Of poverty
Their smiles struck down
Like bullets wounds
Through tambourines
Through presidents

We keep killing our children
Without their mothers permission
Old men sending young boys off to war
With the dying milk
Of this sick patriotism
Smeared all over their conscience;
What of humanity?

Men
Submerged
In the galloping grease
Of this dishonest freedom
This is more
Than lambs fat
Or genocide

Grown men fighting
Over who gets to be buried
In the nicer coffins
How many flags will we raise
Before we realize
That flags
Don't raise children.

Two Sevenths

2/7th of a giraffe's soul fused with the breeding patterns of sperm whales oil spills the spinal chord of a miniature half horse bent to an exact angle syringes filled with poverty dictators and broken emptiness injected into the spines of third world children perspiring poison spoon eating Jesus out of the pores of the H-bomb HBO selling tickets to their lynching language within language torture machines by tortured men five diluted tongues of experimental blame paper money paper god paper people got us believing in ink how much is a dollar worth in gold or diamonds how much is it worth in mothers or children translate that to apples because eventually apple trees die which brings up the question of Ayatollah Hussein Ho Chi Min busboys in the basement of the pentagon serving the poor to the greedy in the basement of the pentagon where they have developed new shapes and new sounds that control dogs and gods sifting deliriously through the dreams of the collective idiot cold blue funeral beautiful military servicemen with their pressed on clay smiles patches of flesh symbols bleeding machine guns scribbled onto the faces of the newly bombed out children holding hands singing in a deep red furrowed field and in the distance a small white farm house fill with pigs with strings attached raining a toothless drum stumble a blood covered century nestled tight in a tiny silver music box Hitler dressed as a napkin stained with grapes prima ballerina style dancing a soft blue hoop a philosophical dimple of military acoustics a blind folded assembly line of politicians puppets and trolls with their nice shiny Harvard brain implants.

910

America

This is going to hurt
Like a power outage
During your abortion
Hurt like the 666
Is now the American flag
Hurt like Adolf Hitler
Came back as CNN
But now the Muslims are the Jews
This is going to hurt like
The holocaust was an independent film
Slavery was a block buster
That made billions for motherfuckers
Hurt like America was a giant gas chamber
But niggers don't burn well
This is going to hurt like the wolf
Ain't coming in sheep clothing;
The wolf is coming as a chain store
Selling FUBU on UPN with a bucket
Of popcorn chicken, a cross and a crack pipe
Doing an info-mercial on how to spread AIDS
In Africa. This is going to hurt
Like pulling a bowling ball backwards
Through your dick
Hurt like a urinary tract infection
In your tear ducts

Don't cry, America

This is going to hurt like the scent of our ancestors'
Blood caked onto the psyche of White
America, hurt like the memories

Locked up in broken bones
Like the steel grin of starvation
The blood covered face in the window
Of colonialism
This is going to hurt
Like a forget you note
To the third world
Like a 14 year old girl
Giving birth to her brother
This is going to hurt
Like a pair of Nikes
Two sizes too small
Crafted from the skull
Of a Chinese sweatshop worker

This is going to hurt like the World
Bank, the IMF, the Center for Disease
Control. hurt like your third eye
In a glass of white milk, hurt
Like the metal in your ankh was mined
By oppressed Africans, hurt like
There is more racism and apartheid
In your engagement diamond
Than in all of South Africa.
This is going to hurt
Like Reagan was playing president
Hurt like George W Bush was also playing
President; Hurt like the connection
Between the opium trade
And the World Trade Center, hurt
Like being double crossed and framed
By hip hop

Hurt like
Iraq
Iran
Afghanistan
Algeria
Nicaragua
Nigeria
Liberia
Lebanon
Lybia
Jamaica
Grenada
Panama
Palestine
Hurt like being double
Crossed and framed
By the CIA

This is going to hurt like Osama
bin Laden lives in New Jersey,
Hurt like Osama bin Laden
Was killed in 1997
Hurt like 911...
F*#k 911
This is going to hurt
Like 1492
1555
1619
1776
1865
This is going to hurt like 3/5, hurt
Like Japanese concentration camps
On American soil,

Hurt like the Tuskegee experiments,
Like small pox, like reservations,
Like the word *Indian*, like genocide;
Hurt like the bullet that killed
Medgar, Malcolm, Kennedy and King
Was fired from the same vocal chords.
This is going to hurt like Nat
Turner was more American than George
Washington, this is going to hurt
Like a black man late
For his own lynching.

This is going to hurt bad
And it's going to hurt good
And ugly and beautiful
But
Most of all it is going to hurt
Because that's how Karma works
America.

I Want To Have A Baby

I want to have a baby, a Prada baby;
a baby by Coco Chanel,
eyes by Versace, hair by Pantene Pro-V
Swatch teeth, Windows XP, Intel chip
Celeron processor…
Not a smart baby, no!

I need a baby with breast implants;
a Botox baby with 22-inch rims
and leather interior
Gatorade blood, Nike swoosh,
Red Cross logo – a baby I can donate
to charity.

I want a baby with deleted scenes,
with global positioning systems.
Not a baby to love, no,
I need a baby that's a trend,
a baby that comes with a cash back
guarantee. I need a baby with a web site,
super-sized with fries on the side.
I am talking about a state of the art baby;
vintage, post modern, digital,
with Voice Recognition,
and a Quartz movement heart. I want
a baby with a retirement plan.

I need a baby
with twelve different ring-tones
with call waiting and text messaging
a glossy over-priced over-hyped

made in Indonesia with slave labour baby.
I need a baby to give me the light
and pass the draw. I need a baby
that's blazing like hip-hop and R&B.
I need a baby with a black album
a baby with a white album
a baby with a grey album –
a baby that's not even a baby;
I need a baby I will believe is a baby
because the baby went platinum.
I need a Che Guevara baby,
a baby that believes in revolution.

No!
I need a baby that believes
in nothing. A vegetarian, tofu-eating baby.
Fat free, low carb, high fibre baby.
I need a baby with nuclear potential
I need something, anything
I need something to keep me
distracted, something to prevent me
from feeling other people's pain,
something to keep me from believing
that this is the best humanity can do.
I need a baby so I don't have to deal
with reality.

Silent Town

Gun metal
Silent town
Eyes
Blazing with a lonesome fever
Tears of a torn woman settling
In Grandpa's war scars
Still fresh from a hundred
Years of cornfields in his dreams.
Men moving mechanically
Fattened with stupidity
The ink still wet under their blades.
The signatures of merchants
Carve their faces,
Manufacture their hatred.
Nobody speaks for
The uniforms are silent.

Dispatches

War

There is
a McDonald's
in Baghdad

Yesterday I

Yesterday
Malcolm's bullet
wounds
were mailed
to Colin Powell

Yesterday II

Yesterday
Nat Turner's
ashes
were mistaken
for Anthrax

Yesterday III

Yesterday
Garvey's Black Star-Liner
was found
in J.Edgar Hoover's
closet

Yesterday IV

Yesterday
Robeson was found
in the Oval Office
tapping
out the Constitution
in code.

Yesterday V

Yesterday
Harriet's musket
was found
in Condoleeza's bed.

Tele-vision

Middle passage billboard
The blood commerce
Of churches
Continents hung from
Bullet trees
Colonialism tight
Around their testicles
Like 27 years Angola bled
Black mothers
With erasers
To their babies faces
Husbands
Mined like diamonds
Hiroshima fever
Yellow Chernobyl
High like powered history
Witch doctor
Spin doctor
Windmill of sorcery
One arm Russian spy
Soviet classroom
Cuban missile crisis
Ethiopian starving from sunshine
From freedom
Democracy and pop music
Communist Kennedy
Bullet wound the size of Vietnam
Razor wire
Drawn through
The feebled mouths
Of newly minted babies

Stretched hollow
With propaganda
The lonely tumorred eyes
Of future fools
A walking autopsy of spirits
The gun making circus of clarity
Of blue confusion
Agent orange choke hold
Handshake, Coke smile
Nations fall because of this
New opium shaped warships
Politicians at war memorials
Stitched to lies
Their tears lay naked
In secret meetings
With swords and whispers
Don't look back America
The new drug of choice
Is fear
And America is so high
I believe I can walk
A cruel striptease of anarchy
Of coups and treason
Of lying presidents
Premiers and prime ministers
The roost has finally
Come home to chicken
Blacked by asbestos
The beheaded dreams
Of bleached hearts
The perfect taxation
Of partriarchy
Can you hear the insipid howling

Of wall street merchants
The lonely parade of empty men
The multi-national side step of reality
Watch them dance
The way they shape-shift
Metal suits of sorrow
Plenty of coffins
This isn't sky
This is illusion
So pretend this prayer for me please
For king George is back
The German furher is back
With maps of stolen shoe shines
Cotton field flings
Sambo me gentle
Slave cough me death
Until I go blind
For Washington is diseased.

Bleed

Bleed a silvered wing
Cotton ball throats
That either sing or run
Or get murdered
Like skulls of cane stalks
Men on blue horses
A cold white killing
Blowing through their hair
No way back to death
So we stand and watch
Spirits under bearded trees
Souls burnt down
To soot and song
Like rows of sweet
Wooden cabins stolen
Wombs of woven women
Stretched from seven foot kettles
Liquid ovens of black survival
Left for dead
Crying mills
Industrial Cinderella
Dark like rivers

Africa black
We sing stone oak
And pray Shango comes
Spitting the voodoo climax
Of change on the wind
To purge the land
To wash eyes open
History

Getting off ships
Plantations babbling
A crude drumming
The bend of stairs
The big house
The small shack
The tears in chains
Hands chopped off
Still clapping at night
To sweat a sound
And pray their gods kill them
Before we do.

Workshop

A circle
Of turning minds;
Whispers, water and melodies,
A silver delight.
Dreams and promises
Bursting unholy, a fever
Braided into the flesh of speech.
Giant universe.
Liquid buckets of prayers,
Logic magic,
Scribbled smiles,
Realities evaporating
Like tangerine elephants,
Gem eyed and silent.
Time splits
Yesterday and Jupiter
Talking paper.
Tell me stories
Of a mouse
Trapped in a blue piano,
Of lights and strings
And pipelines from planets
In your head
Turning your veins into sheet music.
Walk the Ghandi
With perfect timing.
Water whisper a telephone smile,
Radio dream yourself back to life
In a circle
Of turning minds.

Climax

Our climax
will be in the form of time
machines, the gentle breath
of a damp galaxy dancing,
dipped in wet woman motions.
Warm, sweltering, flesh craving,
nimble church girl fingers slowly
spreading thick liquid darkness
with soft gyrating touches;
tearing into the deep flickering
maroon of your forever space
dripping spirit splitting juices.
Grasp me
like a weeping algebraic expression
dying in the pulsating scat
of your shcitzophrenic sex grease;
hot, sticky, feverish, internal sweat
parable, pelvic slave revolt,
orgasmic rebellion:
let me see, feel and taste
the sweet oily spasm
of your vaginal heartbeat
jumping,
the humid ecstasy grips
of your liquid freedom sighs.
Let me dive head first
into the synapse
of your nerve endings.

Move for me, woman,
sneak me into the language

of your salty nipples panting.
Position your tender,
create that divine arc,
that religious dip in your spine
so I can touch your Bermuda
with an unpredictable
Jamacian-Al-Qaeda stroke
that will leave your spinal cord
in your forearm.
Holy water, drink me slow
like heat, like god, call me
Jesus of Nazareth, no;
call me Judas Iscariot
and lie to me, tell me you feel me
in your wisdom teeth,
in your grandmother's dentures,
in your soul's ovaries,
in your bone marrow,
in the prescription in your glasses.
Let's make love
until we switch species.
I'm talking vicious and hard
like molecular physics,
like two stars colliding,
like the death of a universe.
I need neither promise nor illusion,
just the quivering anxiety of Angels,
the strange stir of a brilliant tornado
twisting, turning, bending, screaming
pushing into the moist muscular
flame of your tightened nebula.

Here is the key to my genetics;

make of me what you please,
but please
perspire me an explanation
to why we are here, paint me
a make believe reincarnation,
show me how to tease
the tender switch of your miracle.
How to lick your scars
until they turn into dreams.
Press tight against me, like
the moment between two milliseconds.
Place your petals on my womb,
kiss me as if I am dying
in the aching screams
of your earthquake blooming.
Let me drink the fluid from your
Spinal column.
Collapse, grasp, push, hold,
hold your breath.
Breathe me sweet.
Tell me you've seen me
in old photos,
in dusted memories,
in distant cites,
tell me you know
who I am.

As Sure As

Not sure if there is a God
Not sure if I am alive
only feel centuries communicating
in this surreal curl of existence
This subtle whispering
of bones surrendering light
like ecstatic eyelids laughing
the smothered death of dreams

the eclipse of veins
penetrating needles
under the seductive grasp
of sexual oil strangling motions
electric pulse
of breath falling faithless
magnetic staggering
of a frantic tongue
spirited
beating back and forth

feverishly exhaling steel
trembling lip lung emotions
blue-red the naked
smoke filled tunnels
of screams and daemons
pausing
A barefooted twirl of blood and saliva
bleeding a weeping Jesus
like broken slices of a blue dove
cooing a collapsed April

Not sure if any of this is real
Not sure if today is Saturday
or 1964
but I know that
the music that moves you
is beautiful

Sweet Woman

How slippery is your soul;
can I touch it
and if I did
would it turn me to stone
would I be mesmerized by its magic
charmed by its deep shivering spirals?
If I should slowly slip my fingers through
the thick moist silky sap
of your sweetened centre
glide emotions through
fields of folded flesh
and feel the heat of your naked rapture
the arch of your spine
the soft of your arse
in the palm of my hand
kneading slowly
pressing with sweet patience
suffocating in the echoes of your moans
like a love song with no words
like an orgasm played on a violin
would you flinch or blush
or both?
What does it feel like
the sound of your flesh
the thought, that is...
Does it constantly throb
and dance a circular coil
curled like a slippery seduction
screaming to be released?

Slow

pull me slowly
into the madness of your lap
into your fevered
love song slippery

flesh miracle unclasping
sweet tangled dark watery
insides dreaming plutonium
to lick gospels

from the melody of your thighs
curling moan movements
silent spread of flesh
shivering pearl pulse

flesh tender as forever
apocalypsing limbs
intertwined like brainwaves
soaked in lust

suck me into the madness
of your lap like a sunset-
whispered pelvis, like a blind
musician muted horn

opium den
the liquid sliding
down the needle slow
spoon of you

bubbling to bursting

to shoot you vein wise
Mississippi blue song
juices expanding

this ain't love
this is a beautiful suicide

let me rewrite you pass
my tongue through your arteries
valve a thousand
dip a million unicorns

in kryptonite and race them
through you pass
a cherry gently across your ass.
until your nervous system explodes

into negro spirituals
I would love to rewrite you
on the stem of tomorrow
catch the flesh

echoes nestled in the sweet
of your visible

close your eyes and love me
linguistic blindfold
elephant feathers
dipped in honey and crumpled

angels love me
Kansas City black magic
New Orleans gumbo

Negroid voodoo

bass drum rim-shot
skin stretched
until the mahogany stutters
love me 15 frequencies below

insanity 30 frames per second
turn me to dynamite
we'll become stardust
love me 3.1415926535897

love me until
the humming birds
come covered in purple spasms
flaming chocolate hallelujahs

love me
in scat
in sign language
in mandarin

in footsteps
in braille
love me cubed root
cotton gin

moonshine pie chart
crop circle erotic

love me as if you found
me inside gods g-spot
stealing moons from heaven

until your insides whisper

the Pythagorean theorem
and sweaty crotch music
into moments of me you beautiful
taste the audible apostrophes

surrendering the pirouette
of an almost moan
on the cusp of your yearning
hush and press

all that rebellion
back against me until the strings
bend and burst vibrate
and shake franticly

until we turn the dark inside out
and we both explode into songs...

Strip Club

She's a wish
surrendering
a cello
viola beautiful
scriptures tickled
into her
whole note
liquid spirits
migrating up her, uncoiling
historical spasms
in her sweaty.
She could have been something else.
A sandstone figurine
cut from wind and smoke
flesh doves moving across her abdomen
forgive me invisible
cathedral aflame
star clusters in her lip gloss.
She stirs a blue
lap dance sorcery
memories in her dark
Woman-soft
seduction poemed
in her sweet infinity
spilling spells
a riddled flame in her crotch.
Juju beads
Voodoo lips
sex magic woman
possessed by
a silent symphony

Ife in the hip of you.
Liquid medusa
make me a telepath
point me to the stars
nipples like smoke rings around the sun.
You are Mississippi and Kinshasa
sheet music and gravity
the equator torn in half
rat traps going off in your dreams.
mule dance aborted
in this dark dirge
like a firm black jazz.
Gypsy eyes
can I touch you in analog?
Press parabolas into your pandora
and dance you slow
on a midnight wind
and whisper
a million silver winged butterflies
into your binary code,
speak tongues into your belly
translate you from flesh to Kiswahili
from woman to hallelujah
spread you out beautiful
like a earthquake beneath
a waterfall?
I'll take you down
way down below time
and touch you so deep
your atoms
will need to catch their breath
so deep
the spirit of your clit

will moan djembes
through the dreams
of swans and elephants
in psychedelic face paint
exploding through moons.
I'm talking flesh frequencies
psychosexual landslide
and brain bending luminosities.
We'll need a fan
a sound proof room
five cubes of ice
a sprinkle of salt
a table spoon of honey
and a fist full of sky –
just squeeze god into these sheets
because in two seconds
I'll move in you so gently
your conscience will shift
1/8 of a nano meter
open you up so wide
I could time travel
through your pores
and lay naked
in the juices of your genome
memorize your shivers
and leave finger prints
on your electrons;
give you a burst of passion so warm
and terrifyingly beautiful
that the echoes of your orgasm
will change the pH balance
of the universe.
Messiah woman

inject me with the twilight of your insanity
teeth a sunset into my flesh
babble a lullaby into my spirit
pull centuries through me
because I too
I am desperate and alone
and I'm going to Brooklyn.
And I need someone to touch,
to feel,
to know that I'm real.

We Hope You Enjoyed Reading!
Let us know what you think by sending an e-mail to
books@flippedeye.net

Thank You for buying *The Wolf Who Cried Boy*. If you would like more information about waterways publishing, please join our mailing list online at **www.flippedeye.net.**

Visit our other imprints online:

mouthmark *(poetry)*
www.flippedeye.net/mouthmark

lubin & kleyner *(fiction)*
www.flippedeye.net/lubinandkleyner

waterways *(poetry)*
www.waterways-publishing.com